C000020177

A YEAR OF PROGRAMME PLANNING

By David Saint

Cover Design by Ron Branagan
Illustrations by Phil Driver

© Printforce Limited
British Library Cataloguing in Publication Data
A CIP catalogue record for this book is available from
the British Library

ISBN 0 948834 20 X

CONTENTS

A YEAR OF PROGRAMME PLANNING — INTRODUCTION

This book has been written largely with the needs of leaders of all forms of youth groups in mind. However, we hope that the contents will be of value to anybody involved in planning activities and programmes for a wide range of organisations.

There is nothing new under the sun — there are said to be only six games in the world, and the Chinese reputedly invented all of them! All activities are merely variations on themes, and yet so often, when we have to sit down and plan a programme, the blank page stares back at us, challenging us to think of something exciting — and we can't.

We have made no attempt to write programmes for different ages, or to indicate for which age group a particular programme is meant. We believe that Leaders are already used to adapting ideas from various sources to suit their own circumstances. The intention in this book is to provide ideas to help you build your own programmes, to suit the aims and objectives of your own organisation, to fit the sex(es) and ages of your members, and to take account of your own resources of equipment, finance, accommodation and environment.

The book has been divided into a number of sections. There are suggestions for each month, many referring to specific anniversaries. Then we have sections on wet weather activities, outdoor activities, outings, and panic programmes, to suit those occasions where the best laid plans of mice and men .... you know the sort of thing we mean. There is a section in which we have taken 12 themes and developed them, partly for you to use as they are, and partly as a model to show how almost any of the other ideas in this book could be similarly expanded.

We have, as a rule, not given details of particular games to fit in with the programmes, as these are generally readily found in a number of books which are widely available. Most games, especially when used with the under 11s, can be adapted to suit the theme of the day, with a simple alteration of story line.

There are a number of occasions when we suggest inviting speakers. It is *vital* that you make sure the speaker knows the audience age group and size, the subject of his talk and the time limit. A good speaker can provide a welcome change — a bad speaker can be disastrous.

Happy Programme Planning!

PLANNING SKILLS

Successful programme planning depends on the use of a number of skills.

- **Imagination** on the part of the Leader is essential if the imagination of the members is to be captured.
- **Balance**, both in the overall programme for the year and in each individual programme is vital if the interest of the youngsters is to be maintained, and if your objective for them is to be achieved.
- **Flexibility** is important, so that programmes can be adapted, often at the last minute, to suit circumstances arising, or to take advantage of current events.
- **Organisation** will enable you to progress through your plans without those panic-stricken moments when you realise a piece of equipment is missing, or you have forgotten to book a hall.
- **Delegation**, perhaps the hardest skill of all to master, makes it possible for you to maintain more of an overview of what is going on, to be able to react to problems as they arise and to be able to see how things could be improved in the future. It also gives your Assistants

a chance to try their hand, show what they can do and build up their confidence and experience so that, one day, when you hang up your Programme Planning Chart for good, they can step comfortably into your shoes.

Planning a programme is like making a cake. A number of different ingredients are needed, each in the right quantities, with perhaps a little spice added 'to taste'. When planning a weekly programme, and looking at it as part of a year's programme, ask yourself if you have enough of the right ingredients and whether there is perhaps a little too much of your own favourite tipple!

Is there plenty of:

Fun   Learning experience
Physical activity   Character development
Challenge   Creativity

Are there opportunities for:

Learning about   Religious experience
  personal relationships   Helping others
Learning about oneself   Self discipline

THEMES

It is not always essential to have a theme for one meeting, or for a month of meetings, but there are advantages in using this method of planning occasionally. It makes it easier for the planner in some ways, as there is a 'peg' on which to hang ideas and a line of thought to follow. A theme also helps the youngsters to feel a sense of continuity, to feel more involved and to let their imaginations work along specific lines. The disadvantages are that, unless the programme is carefully planned and the items well broken up, it can become boring. Some of the links can become more than a little tenuous, which can undermine the effectiveness of the whole idea.

Almost any subject, or object, can be developed as a theme, as long as the pitfalls are carefully avoided. In this section we have given 12 themes and listed a number of ideas for each. Not all the ideas will be appropriate for your circumstances but then you would not use all of them anyway! Simply select those which appeal and are suitable, develop them to suit your members, then build your programme around them.

At the end of the section we have listed a large number of other possible themes for you to develop in your own way.

Water

- Organise a visit to a local lock, pumping station or dam.
- Carry out some simple water science experiments.
- Water fights are always popular! Squeezy bottles, balloons or good old fashioned water pistols all make good weapons. Make sure you have a large bucket of water for your own self protection!
- Learn about methods of collecting water and purifying it for drinking.
- Try a new water sport — water polo, canoeing, fishing, surfing or sailboarding under supervision.
- Make a simple boat, either a toy or a lifesize one.
- Visit the local boating lake — you should be able to negotiate special rates for a block-booking.
- Invite a weather forecaster or a representative of the British Waterways Board to come and give a talk.

Literature

A stuffy subject? It all depends on the presentation.

- Visit a local literary location, preferably with someone who can enthuse knowledgeably about it.
- Hold a book sale, or book swapping session, or set up a library for your group with books donated by the members. Appoint a librarian who should seek advice from his public library on how to carry out his duties.
- Invite a local writer to come and talk to the group. If you do not know of one, the local paper should be able to tell you.
- Invite a carefully selected book enthusiast to come and tell the members why he or she finds books so absorbing.
- Produce a list of famous quotations and invite small groups of youngsters to act out the scene.
- Play 'Give Us a Clue', in which one team is given the name of a book, play, film etc. and they have to mime it to the other teams until somebody guesses it.
- Hold a literary quiz.
- Invite members (having given hem a couple of weeks' notice) to review a book for the rest of the group, in not more than 3 minutes.

Leisure

As more and more of us have more and more leisure time to fill, it can be no bad thing to give a little thought to the ways we fill it.

- Organise a number of 'workshops' on various hobbies, each manned by a Leader, helper or parent, or representatives of local clubs. Small groups of members spend, say 10 minutes at one workshop, then move on to the next.
- Having allowed a few weeks' notice for preparation, invite some of your members to give a talk on, or better still, a demonstration of their hobby.
- Sit all the members down in front of a large sheet of paper or blackboard and have a 'think tank' to list as many hobbies or pastimes as possible. Each member then selects one which is new to them, gets involved in it over, say, the next 4 weeks, then reports back with a 2 minute talk on their experiences.

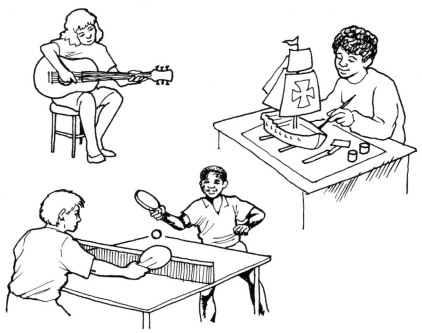

- Ask the members, in small groups, to invent a new game, using only one item of equipment such as a match box or quoit, then play each of them in turn, with the inventors running their own games.
- Have a debate on the use of leisure time and how it is developing into the end of the century.
- Having forewarned them, ask a number of members to give a one minute review of a television programme they have enjoyed, a book they have read or a film or show they have seen.
- Conduct a survey into how people spend their leisure time. Do not confine it to your own members, but try to explore the different amounts of time available and the different uses of that time by different age groups.
- Design a leisure park or adventure playground.
- For a really silly 10 minutes, supply a number of toys quite unsuited to the age group and let them play with them. 7–11 year olds, for example, might surprise you with the way they cope with sophisticated and complicated equipment enjoyed by their older brothers and sisters. Give 12–16 year olds some of the toys intended to teach toddlers basic skills and some of them might have some difficulty coping with them. Hand a box of Lego to the over 16's and you might never be able to make them go home!

Charity

'The poor are always with us'. In fact, the activities of thousands of charities throughout the country mean that they are seldom far from us. In some ways this is counter-productive, as we start to build protective barriers and often don't notice yet another appeal for help or money.

• Give each group two weeks to find out about a charity of their choice and then report back about it to the meeting, for about 3 minutes.
• Invite a speaker from a local charity, preferably one selected by your members.
• Visit a local home or centre for the handicapped or elderly. Avoid allowing the children to treat those they are visiting as 'goldfish' to be stared at. See if there is some real way the youngsters can offer assistance, if possible to the people themselves, rather than to the 'fabric' of the place.
• Through games and activities, help the children experience disabilities. Use blindfolds, borrow ear defenders from a hire shop or building firm to simulate a hearing handicap, carry out games and activities using only one hand, or without standing up. A lot of the results will seem funny to the children. Help them to understand it is not so funny for people with those disabilities for life.
• Discuss aids for disabled people, possibly arising out of the above activity. Design a toy for a child who cannot see, or who cannot use his hands.
• Have a discussion on ways your organisation could help other people. Try to build something positive on one or two of the suggestions.
• Invite a 'child orientated' local Vicar to come and talk to the youngsters about the ethics of charity.

Food

A theme dear to everybody's heart, yet how much do we really know about it?

- Invite a dietician to talk to the group and have a discussion about members' favourite foods.
- Make things to eat.
- Try different forms of outdoor cooking.
- Plan menus for specific occasions — childrens' parties, a 21st Birthday, Mother's Day etc.
- Carry out an exercise in costing food, using newspaper advertisements or a visit to the supermarket for information.
- Explore food from around the world and, if possible, have some demonstrations (and samplings) of cooking from other cultures.
- Produce a survey of favourite and most disliked foods. Examine the common factors.
- Learn about the diets of people living in the Third World. Examine ways of doing something to help.
- Learn about survival foods. Plan what emergency rations to take on a five day expedition.

Transport

A theme to which everybody can relate.

- Supply the members with the components to design and build a vehicle. For the under 11s there might be cotton reels, rubber bands, assorted boxes, bits of wood and wire and so on. For those up to late teenage more sophisticated equipment might include gear wheels, a battery operated motor etc. Those over 16 or so might produce something quite significant with bits of old lawn-mower, a pram chassis etc. In each case the vehicle should be a team effort, must be designed and build against the clock and must work!
- Arrange a demonstration, according to age, of road safety, cycle safety or driving techniques, by a policeman, Road Safety Officer, driving instructor etc.
- Arrange a demonstration, including practical work, of cycle or car maintenance.
- Arrange a visit to a bus garage, railway workshop, airport, port, car assembly plant.
- Supply the members with a list of destinations and a number of timetables. Ask them to plan routes to those destinations from your meeting place, using public transport. They should supply as much information as possible, including times, prices etc.
- Arrange with a neighbouring group, or within your own organisation, chariot races, a sedan chair rally or rickshaw races. In any case, the competitors should build their own vehicles.
- Ask one of your members, or a parent, to give a talk about his hobby or train spotting, motor racing, vintage cars etc.
- Hold a glider or hot-air balloon competition, with the members making their own devices once again.
- Organise or take part in a BMX rally, car rally, or skateboarding or roller skating event.
- Making sure all components are labelled with their owners' names, set up a co-operative Scalextric evening!

Nature

How often do we really stop and look at the other world which goes on all around us?

- Go on a nature trail. Have a nature photograph or drawing competition. Have a talk by a local naturalist.
- This will take a lot of careful planning but a Pets Corner, either populated by members' own pets or from a local zoo etc., would be very popular, especially if someone was on hand to give out information and advice.
- It is often said that the camel looks as though it was designed by a committee. Ask groups of youngsters to get together to 'design' the perfect 20th Century pet, just for fun!
- Make leaf or bark rubbings, or take paw prints.
- Gardening is usually regarded as a boring chore by youngsters, usually under the influence of their parents! If you have the space, set up your own little garden, even if it is only a window box, and let the members take a full part in planning its use and tending it. Alternatively, experiment with some of the simple 'window sill gardening' activities like bulbs in pots, mustard and cress, alfalfa etc.
- Visit a zoo, garden, conservatory, arboretum, aquarium etc.
- Make bird boxes, rabbit hutches, a glass case for an ant colony, a fish tank.
- Carry out a survey of the flora and fauna in and around your meeting place. You might be surprised, if not appalled!

Travel and Geography

Back to school? Hardly!

- Obtain a world map. Mark on it places of origin of your members, where people they know live, where they have been on holiday etc. See how many connections your group has with the wider world, without realising it.
- Perhaps using the same map, plus a wealth of travel literature etc., invite each group of members to decide where they, as a group, would like to go, and why. This will be an exercise in co-operation and compromise if nothing else!
- Collect a number of competition entry forms from cereal packets, soap products and the like, and make some group entries to try to win foreign holidays etc. it would be an idea to decide before you start what to do if you win — you never know!
- Give each team a list of specific questions about one country, a number of reference books and 10 minutes to find the answers.
- Invite a speaker from another country, or a travel firms, or simply a well travelled person, especially if their travel was for an interesting reason, such as missionary work, or on government business.

Entertainment

- Hold a talent evening, with or without warning, and see what your members are capable of. Do not force anybody to have a go but encourage those who wish to take part.
- Make musical instruments — their complexity will depend on the age range — and play some simple tunes.
- Have a competition to write a topical song. It may be helpful to give some suggestions as to topics and/or tunes.
- Write a topical comedy sketch. It should be possible to be at least as good as those on T.V.!
- Visit a circus, local amateur dramatics show etc.
- Stage your own circus by and for the youngsters. No animals, but plenty of acrobatics and clowning.
- As an extra surprise bring in a childrens' entertainer at the end of the evening.
- Bring in a honky-tonk pianist and get them all singing!
- Hold a joke telling competition — find the best, and the worst!
- Arrange for the use of a record player, then invite members to bring their favourite record, play one minute of it, say something about it and why they like it.
- Our other publications — Campfire Stunts, Campfire Stunts II, Campfire Songs, On With Your Show and Let's Act should give you plenty of useful material for Entertainment Evenings.

Health

Not a subject dear to the heart of the average child perhaps but still one which is worth looking at.

- Sample a range of health foods. If possible, have somebody to talk about them. Try to avoid the lunatic fringe — you may have parents asking awkward questions!
- Bring in a P.E. or Keep Fit instructor to demonstrate and explain some simple exercises.
- Have a health quiz to get across some basic hygiene rules in a fun way.
- Hold a discussion on the topic 'Prevention is Better than Cure'.
- Invite a local doctor, dentist, midwife, chemist or brain surgeon to come and give a short talk, preferably without illustrations!
- Have a 'Think Tank' to list health hazards. See if any lessons can be learned.

Language

Perhaps the most basic of human skills and certainly one we give the least thought to.

- Try to learn some sign language or ask a teacher from a special school to teach the children some of the signs used for severely disabled children.
- Learn a little Esperanto.
- Provide the members with a list of common words and phrases and some reference books. Ask them to translate them into several languages, then compare them. Don't forget to include American!
- Invite a foreign language speaker who can also cope with English to come and give the children an idea of what a foreign language should really sound like and what it really means.
- Hold an evening in which only French (or at a stretch Franglais) is spoken.
- Find out what other languages can be spoken by the members, even if it is only a few words.
- Obtain some foreign newspapers or books, especially illustrated ones, and see what the members can make of them. Have a few dictionaries handy, perhaps.

Paperclips

(Just to show a programme really can be built around any subject!)

- Invite each youngster to make a paperclip sculpture. Other materials could be used in addition, but the predominant ingredient should be paperclips.
- Ask the teams to invent a better paperclip (and the best of luck!)
- Distribute a limited number of paperclips in unusual places about the meeting room before the children arrive. Have a paperclip treasure hunt.
- Make a fishing game with cardboard fish with paperclips attached, part protruding, and canes as fishing rods with paperclip hooks. See who can catch the most!
- See how many words of 3 letters or more each individual can make from the word PAPERCLIP.
- Cut out squares of paper about 6" in size. Write large numbers on them 1–5, and attach them to a line suspended at a suitable height across the meeting place, using paperclips of course. Give a question and five possible answers, then call out a number. The member of each team who has been given that number runs out and tries to be the first to pluck off the correct numbered card relating to the correct answer and brings it to you.

- As a handcraft session make decorative bookmarks with a large paperclip attached securely to the back to stop it slipping out of the book.
- Have a competition to see who can make the most convincing large paperclip out of a wire coat hanger. Well, it's one way to get rid of them!
- Using paperclips as templates, see who can make the most original sketch. As with the sculpture, the largest proportion of the lines must relate to the paperclip, although a few extras could be allowed.

Ideas of themes for you to develop:

Housebricks	Photography
Telephones	Old age
Communication	Computers
The Romans	Electricity
Flight	Democracy
Worship	Do It Yourself
Inventions	Cartoons
Fashion	Churches
Newspapers	String
Architecture	Music
Wood and woodworking	Stamps
Humour	Radio
Unusual sports	Numbers
Maps	The Bible
Time	

MONTH BY MONTH IDEAS

On the following pages we set out a large number of possible themes and other ideas which you can use as a 'peg' for programme planning. They act both as a 'springboard' for your own imagination and as an opportunity to remind the youngsters of certain events and people, and to help them learn something about them or what they are associated with, in the format of an enjoyable evening of games, creativity and action.

Rather than leave you stranded with these rather bald lists of events, we have also set out some suggestions for developing one of the themes for each month. We show how even an unpromising idea can become a useful basis for planning a programme that will appeal to your members and help them develop. This process can be applied to any of the ideas suggested.

January

1 New Year's Day
Britain entered Common Market (1973)
4 Jacob Grimm born (1785). Compiler of fairy tales
Louis Braille born (1809). Invented Braille
Sir Isaac Pitman born (1813). Developed shorthand
6 Montgolfier born (1745). Hot air balloonist
9 First Concorde trial flight (1969)
10 Penny Post introduced (1840)
14 Cecil Beaton born (904). Photographer
18 A.A. Milne born (1882). Wrote the 'Pooh' books
19 James Watt born (1736). Invented the steam engine
20 Is the date of the inauguration of the President of the U.S.A.
every 4 years
24 Hadrian born (76 B.C.). Built Hadrian's Wall
25 Burn's Night (Robert Burns born 1759)
26 Australia Day
27 First public demonstration of T.V. by John Logie Baird (1926)
Lewis Carroll born (1832). Wrote Alice in Wonderland
The Victoria Cross instituted (1856)

There is often snow about in January. Help those who cannot enjoy the snow by shopping for the elderly or clearing their front paths.

This is a difficult time for animals and birds. See if you can help them by leaving suitable foodstuffs where they can get at them without being molested. Watch and see who helps himself.

January — The introduction of the Penny Post. Arrange a visit to a Post Office or a talk by a representative of the Post Office. Have a stamp swapping session or invite someone to show and talk about some of their collection of stamps. Play a variation on the game of He, in which the Royal Mail has to get through, despite the best endeavours of brigands and highway men! Play a memory game involving British place names. Give members a picture stamp each and invite them to tell a story for 1 minute, inspired by the stamp.

February

6 New Zealand Day
     Accession of Queen Elizabeth II
7 Charles Dickens born (1812)
8 Jules Verne born. (Author of Round the World in 80 Days, Journey to the Centre of the Earth etc.)
9 Next appearance of Halley's Comet — 1986
14 St. Valentine's Day
15 Galileo, astronomer, born (1564)
22 Robert Baden-Powell born (1857)
23 Samuel Pepys, diarist, born
29 Leap Year only

March

1 St. David's Day
3 Alexander Graham Bell born (1847). Invented the telephone
     Sir Henry Wood born (1869). Instituted the Promenade Concerts
17 St. Patrick's Day
     Popularly regarded during the Middle Ages as the day Noah entered the Ark
31 The Eiffel Tower inaugurated (1889)

February — Charles Dickens born. Devise a game of pickpockets and detectives (a la Fagin). Play a game in which members have to grab "Scrooge's" money without him turning round to see them. Forewarn the members and ask them to bring the most unusual object they can find for your own Old Curiosity shop.

Ask each team to enact a scene from a Dickens book of their own choice. Supply them with copies of his works for reference. Dickens was a great descriptive writer. Give the youngsters an opportunity to try their hand at descriptive writing, particularly about actual people.

March — 17th, the day Noah was said to have entered the Ark. Make a model of the Ark on mount Ararat. Make models or drawings of animals. Devise a game in which Noah has to catch the animals to go into the Ark. (The mind boggles at the task!) Give the youngsters the chance to do some role play — one as Noah having been warned of the Flood and the others as the disbelieving rest of Humanity. Try transplanting the situation to the present day. How would our friends and neighbours react! Have another look at the Bible story and perhaps also at similar stories and traditions from other religions and cultures. Devise a quiz on animal names and habits.

April

1   April Fool's Day
    Royal Air Force formed (1918)
2   Hans Christian Andersen born (1805)
4   Sir Francis Drake knighted (1581)
    Grinling Gibbons, sculptor, born (1648)
6   Houdini, escapologist and magician, born (1874)
7   World Health Organisation established (1948)
9   Brunel, engineer, born (1806)
12 Yuri Gagarin became first man in space (1961)
14 Cuckoo day, when the first cuckoo is traditionally heard
16 Charlie Chaplin born (1889)
20 Rome founded by Romulus (735 B.C.)
21 Moonwalk (1972)
23 St. George's Day
    Shakespeare born (1564)
27 Samuel Morse, inventor of Morse Code, born (1791)

    Activities to prepare for camping season
    Cycling and cycle safety
    Weather — there is plenty of variety this month!

May

1   May Day
12 Edward Lear born (1812). Famous for his nonsense poems
13 Sir Arthur Sullivan born (1842)
17 Mafeking relieved (1900)
21 Elizabeth Fry born (780). Social worker and prison reformer
22 Sir Arthur Conan Doyle born (1859)
26 John Wayne born (1907)
28 Ian Fleming born (1908). Creator of James Bond
30 Joan of Arc burned at the stake (1431)

    Morris dancing. Maypole dancing, hobby horse festival

April — Grinling Gibbons (sculptor) born in 1648. Although he is a very famous sculptor, paradoxically little is known about him. Find out if any of his works can be seen in your area and go and visit them. Perhaps encourage your members to research into his work — what copies there are available today, where his creations are, who he made them for originally. Build on the theme of sculpture and have an evening of creativity, with different bases for different material including clay, metal, woodcarving (observing safety precautions of course), Origami, junk sculpture etc.

May — 12th, Edward Lear born. The found of limericks and famous for his nonsense verse, Edward Lear could provide an hilarious theme for an evening. Punctuated with readings from his works, an evening could include a limerick competition, rewriting parts of the training programme or ceremonies as nonsense verse (if this is skilfully led it will require careful thought about the subject matter by the members.) Play a variety of absurd games. Perhaps play more common games but with absurd rules, like football, in which you must not score a goal, or Kim's Game in which all the objects are given each others' names, just to confuse things.

June

2 Queen Elizabeth II crowned (1953)
9 George Stephenson born (1781). The Rocket
11 John Constable, landscape artist, born (1776)
Jacques Cousteau, undersea explorer, born (1910)
19 Sir Robert Peel's Act for establishing the Police Force passed
21 First stone laid for the re-building of St. Paul's Cathedral by Sir Christopher Wren
24 Midsummer's Day
Feast of the birthday of St. John the Baptist

Midsummer Madness
Water safety ready for summer holidays

July

1 Investiture of the Prince of Wales (1969)
4 U.S. Independence Day
(Doctor) Thomas Barnardo born (1845)
5 1841 — the first excursion organised by Thomas Cook
The Salvation Army founded (1865)
12 Julius Caesar born (100 B.C.)
14 Bastille Day in France
Emmeline Pankhurst born (1858)
15 Inigo Jones, architect, born (1573)
Rembrandt born (1606)
First issue of Punch published (1842)
20 Lunar module lands on moon (1969)
21 Neil Armstrong walked on the moon (1969)
Paul Julius Von Reuter born (1816). Started Reuters News Agency
28 Beatrix Potter born (1866)
29 The first Scout camp, on Brownsea Island, started in 1907
30 Henry Ford born (1863)

Photography and map reading, in preparation for holidays

June — John Constable born, on the 11th, in 1776. Provide the materials and a view and see if you have any budding Constables in the group. Show reproductions of two or three Constables (if the originals are not readily to hand) and then run a quiz on them. Obtain small reproductions or postcards, cut them up and have a Constable Jigsaw Relay. Tell the group a story inspired by one of the pictures. Be brave, make it up as you go along. Invite a local painter to come and talk to the group about techniques for painting.

July — The first issue of Punch published. This is another opportunity for an amusing evening. Provide cartoons, particularly from Punch, without their captions. Members to invent their own. If you have any cartoonists in the group, give them a chance to show their skill. If you can get one, ask a cartoonist to come and show you the tricks of the trade. Punch also contains amusing articles and parodies, particularly of current events. Ask the team to write a rather more amusing version of the day's news than appears in the papers. Supply papers for reference. Invite them to write their version of one of your programme planning meetings. Use back numbers of Punch for wordsearch games or other contests.

August

9   Thomas Telford born (1757). Builder of roads, bridges and canals
16 The Tate Gallery opened (1897)
17 The first gold discovered in the Klondyke (1896)
    Davey Crockett, frontiersman, born (1786)
22 The first public television transmission in Britain (1932)
26 Julius Caesar landed in Britain (55 B.C.)

This is a good month for outdoor activities, such as hikes, pioneering and barbecues

September

1   Edgar Rice Burroughs born (2875). Creator of Tarzan
2   1666 — Great Fire of London began
6   The first British Telephone Exchange opened
15 Battle of Britain Day
17 Sir Francis Chichester born
19 George Cadbury, founder of the sweet firm, born (1839)
23 The George Cross initiated (1940)
29 Nelson born (1758)

August — The start of the Klondyke Gold Rush in 1896. Why not organise a gold rush event of your own. There are plenty of ingredients here for an adventurous day out — treasure hunting, survival andbackwoodsmanship, keen competition and rivalry, breakneck races, wagons, ambushes — what potential .....!

September — **2nd** — Great Fire of London. Visit the Monument, near where it all started. Visit the local Fire Station or have a talk by a Fire Prevention Officer. Try out, under carefully controlled conditions, fire extinguishers, fire blankets etc. Practice the Fireman's Chairlift. Look at fire safety drill for your meeting place. Organise games on the theme of preventing or escaping from fire.

October

1	1869 — The first postcards on sale (in Austria)
4	Orville Wright's pioneering flight (1905)
9	Captain Cook first lands in New Zealand (1769)
14	Battle of Hastings (1066)
15	Florence Nightingale born (1820)
20	Sir Christopher Wren born (1632)
25	St. Crispin's Day (Patron Saint of Shoemakers)
31	Halloween National Magic Day (mainly observed in USA), to commemorate the death of Houdini in 1926

November

1	The first part of Britain's first Motorway, the M1, opened in 1959
5	Guy Fawkes Night
11	Remembrance Day
13	Robert Louis Stevenson born (1830). Wrote Treasure Island
30	St. Andrew's Day

December

5	Walt Disney born (1901)
8	James Thurber born (1894), creator of the Walter Mitty character
10	Human Rights Day
16	The Boston Tea Party (1773)
21	The first crossword puzzle published in the New York World (1913)
30	Rudyard Kipling born (1805). Creator of the Jungle Book stories

Christmas handcrafts
Carol singing

October — St. Crispin's Day, October 25th. St. Crispin is the Patron Saint of Shoemakers. Have a talk by a shoemaker, cobbler or shoe salesman. Visit a shoemaker's. Invite your members to design shoes for different occasions. Look at suitable footwear for expeditions, hikes, mountaineering etc. Play games requiring substantial use of the feet. Try your hand at 'wellie throwing'!

November — The M1 was opened in 1959. Have a route planning competition, making extensive use of motorways. Supply maps for the purpose. Give the members an opportunity to study a map and then recommend where they would put the next motorway (and how they would pay for it!?). The central reservations are now becoming unplanned nature reserves as they are generally inaccessible to the public. Find out about some of the wildlife that is colonising them. Devise a game based on motorway signs.

December — The creator of Walter Mitty was born. Walter Mitty was a character who constantly imagined he was some other, usually heroic, person. Here is a great opportunity for play acting, mime, invention, character creation and humour. To set the scene, read one of, or part of one of, the Walter Mitty stories to the group first.

PANIC!

We all have those occasions when we are not as prepared as we might have been, or when circumstances overtake us. We are suddenly lumbered with a meeting we did not expect to run, we are short of helpers or we are let down. This section is intended to help in two ways. First, by making suggestions as to how to be prepared for at least some eventualities and second, by offering some ready-made ideas that need little or no preparation and little or no equipment.

Prepare Yourself

• A panic box is a wonderful device which should be carried at all times. Without being made too bulky or heavy, it should be filled with some carefully selected paraphernalia which can be used in a number of ways for instant games.

These items might include a set of blindfolds, a packet of balloons, pencils and paper, two tennis balls, a newspaper, sellotape, some empty yoghurt tubs, 10 assorted small items for identification or memory games and a 'crib sheet' to remind you of all those simple but enjoyable games you need in a moment of panic.

• Compile a list of people you can call upon in an emergency — before you need them. Tell them they are on your list and why. They may be retired leaders or leaders from other organisations, friends, parents of members or people with some specific skill.
• Keep careful records of your programmes, with notes on their success. This will become an ever expanding resource of ideas which you already know and understand, but of which you may just need a reminder.

- Make full use of delegation, not just to your assistants and helpers but also to the older members of your groups. In this way, if one or two people let you down, the effect is minimised.
- Whatever you plan, think it through again carefully to find out what could go wrong, then plan accordingly. Ask your most pessimistic friend to help you! Even if nothing does go wrong, you can use your contingency plans on some other occasion, so nothing is wasted!

Instant ideas

- Television games (i.e. games shown on TV) are always good fun to play in meetings and have the advantage that they do not usually need to be explained to the youngsters first. These will include 'What's My Line', in which competitors have to guess the occupations of guests (members could be nominated to represent a particular job); 'Give Us a Clue', in which competitors try to tell their colleagues the name of a film, book etc., through mime alone; 'Just a Minute', in which competitors have to talk for one minute on a given topic without deviating, hesitating or repeating themselves. There are, of course, many others.
- Organise a Scavenger Hunt, in which the youngsters have to find items on a list you supply, or items beginning with a certain letter, or of a certain colour etc.
- Cut up a number of postcards and scatter the pieces about, hiding them. Hold a jigsaw treasure hunt.
- How often do your members have a story read to them? Give them a treat!
- Invite the members to set and break records. Some might be the usual long jump, high jump etc., others might be less traditional, like standing on one leg, seeing how many people can balance on a housebrick etc. Check the Guinness Book of Records for ideas!
- Prepare a set of envelopes, each containing challenges of various types, some silly and some taxing. Members pick an envelope and see how they get on!
- Ask members to relate their favourite shaggy dog stories. Hot drinks should be supplied to keep everybody awake!
- Organise some Wacky Races — 3 handed egg and spoon race, obstacle course in a sack, blindfold baton relays, backwards dribbling

(of footballs!) etc.

• Ask your members to write a job description for yourself, your assistants and the other leaders in your organisation. An exercise in seeing ourselves as others see us!

• Emergency! Dream up a number of emergency situations and allow teams a very limited time to decide how to react. For example, they come across a serious car accident. There is no sign of the emergency services and the crowd of onlookers seems unwilling to get involved. Two minutes to decide what to do. Smoke is coming from the upstairs window of a house. One minute to decide what to do. Whilst walking through a store you see somebody take something off a shelf and put it in their pocket. 1 minute to decide what to do.

• Make a list of five or six different ball games and organise a fast-moving evening of knockout competitions.

OUTDOOR ACTIVITIES

We do not offer programmes as such in this section, as requirements will vary widely according to the time available to you, the time of year and the geography of your surroundings. The intention here is to offer a range of suggestions of things to try. Again, no new ideas but perhaps some activities that would not immediately spring to mind.

- Make and fly kites. Do not be limited by the old fashioned 'kite' shape but experiment with others.
- Take a few well presented reference books and, if possible, some binoculars and go bird-watching near a local wooded area. Over a short period this will generally appeal to more children than one might imagine.
- Stage an emergency and see how the youngsters react. It might be an incident which is clearly staged for their benefit, such as a simulated injury, or it might appear to be a genuine incident sprung on them by surprise, such as people escaping from a house burglary or a small child having got lost. Although these exercises are very valuable in helping youngsters to be able to deal with emergency situations, which would be applauded by the emergency services, you must advise those services of your plans before-hand, in case a member of the public sees your 'emergency' and calls the police or the ambulance out on a fool's errand. They would not be applaud then!
- If you have a suitably wooded area where fires can be lit safely and with permission, experiment with different kinds of wood for firelighting and cooking. Alternatively, collect wood from a number of different locations and use it at a more convenient place.
- Build alternative housing — a mud hut, tepee, log cabin, bivouac — even an igloo!
- Having carried out research with your members, spend a day recreating living conditions from the past, such as the Stone Age.

- Before the meeting, take a number of photographs of the area in which your activity is to be held, each from an unusual or unlikely angle. Give a set of these pictures to each team and a set of markers on cocktail sticks. The teams have to ascertain where each photograph was taken from, then place the marker at that spot, indicating the direction you were facing. Make sure you can remember the answers!
- Have a sandcastle competition. Even if there is no sand for miles around, you can buy a couple of sacks of 'sandpit sand' from builders' merchants for a modest sum. Great fun can be had by all!
- Try grass sledging down a fairly steep but unobstructed hill. Make sure there are no boulders or sudden drops and that there is a safe stopping area at the bottom. Sledges can be specially made or old tin trays can be used as an excellent substitute.
- Find a suitable area for hiding, then give all the members 10 minutes not just to hide but to actually camouflage themselves. Award points both for successful hiding and also for ingenuity in camouflage. In case they are too good you had better arrange a signal, such as a whistle blast, to indicate that the exercise is over and they should come out of hiding!
- Go blackberrying. The harvest can either be used by the members to make something or taken home to their mums or given to a suitable local home.
- Set up an obstacle course.
- Create an Agatha Christie type 'scene-of-the-crime' for the members to investigate. Leave lots of foot-prints, tyre tracks, cigarette ends, broken twigs — all the usual paraphernalia of mystery stories and ask the members to see what they can deduce from the scene.

Make sure there are lots of clues including a few unusual ones and some red herrings. Planning this becomes easier if you decide in your own mind what did happen, then arrange the clues accordingly, rather than dumping a number of effects in a pile and leaving the sleuths to get on with it!
- Go foraging for natural handcraft materials, either to use now or later in the winter. Pebbles for painting, shells, leaves and flowers to dry, holy leaves for Christmas decorations, feathers, fir cones, bits of twig or driftwood — there is a wealth of useful material just waiting to be

picked up.

- If you have a suitable area of fairly loose bare earth, or sand, have a real treasure hunt. Bury a box of sweets, give the youngsters a map and spades and forks, then sit back and enjoy yourself. If you are really sneaky, it might be a good way to get your potato bed dug over!

OUTINGS

It is not the purpose of this book to advise on running outings but rather to make suggestions for you to build on. To this end, we list a number of possible places to take your gang to. The list itself may spark off many more ideas of your own. Just remember 2 golden rules. Make sure you are expected and make sure you and your members know what is expected of you.

• Many places of business and providers of services are only too happy to show round parties of young people, both from the point of view of publicising their work and with an eye to possible recruits for the future. The main drawback is that you may have to fit in with the times they offer you. It might also be necessary to limit the numbers in any one party. The advantage of a pre-arranged visit is that somebody knowledgeable will usually show you around and supply a lot of background information and you will often be shown areas not normally open to the public.

• Consider some of these: The Post Office, Police or Fire Stations, a bank, factory or railway workshop. Carefully researched and planned visits to the Town Hall, library, local church or technical college or university can be very interesting.

• Nature subjects are always popular. The zoo is an obvious suggestion but how about a local vet or animal sanctuary, boarding kennels, farm, gardens (including particularly spectacular private ones), arboretum or conservatory. And don't forget the small private zoos and animal collections.

• Creative work is always fascinating to watch and learn about and their proponents are usually more than willing to welcome spectators. Visit a pottery, glassworks, artist's studio, a rope maker, photographic studio, film studio or carpenter.

• There is plenty to see at the docks, in a garage, at a dairy, at the telephone exchange and at a newspaper office. Many military establishments will give conducted tours but some are only accessible on Open Days. Parks are always open and many have more to interest you than grass and flowers. Ask the park keeper to tell your party something about the history of the park and the buildings and artefacts in it.

- Visit a local place of historic interest, again with a knowledgeable guide if one is available.
- Small local museums are often more appealing than the large National ones, as the exhibits are easier to relate to. And don't forget natural features such as rivers, lakes, mountains and moors.
- It is well worth obtaining local guide books, directories such as the National Trust List of Properties and local maps, to find worthwhile places to visit.
- Why not organise a fact hunt? Select an area with plenty of interest and compile, with expert help if you need it, a list of 20 or more questions which can be answered only by a careful exploration of the area. Set the team loose with the questionnaire. They will learn a lot more than just the answers to your questions.

WET WEATHER ACTIVITIES

When it pours with rain and you had planned an outdoor activity, what do you do?

First, don't panic. Think through the activity and ask yourself whether it really matters if you all get wet. If there is a good chance of pneumonia all round, forget it, but if it just means that you will all get a little bit muddier, quite a lot wetter and that the hot drink at the end of the day will be that much more welcome, if also more diluted, then go ahead!

But let us suppose that common sense prevails, which it seems to do so much these days. Let us prepare for an indoor activity instead.

The most obvious alternative is an indoor version of what you were going to do outside. You were going to play football? Set up a large table top, mark it out and have a blow-football knockout contest instead. You were going to do some pioneering? Go ahead, do some mini-pioneering with garden canes, string and rubber bands, or even cocktail sticks and cotton. Were you looking forward to burnt offerings from the open fire? Invade a kitchen and produce something a little more up-market instead. Or do some mini-cooking, boiling water in eggshells and the like.

Indoor versions of outdoor activities always seem more tame, of course, but the youngsters will understand and will probably be grateful that you have planned something as an alternative! You could make a model camp site, complete with tents, camp kitchens, wet pits etc., using the mini-pioneering techniques above, plus plenty of cardboard and glue. Tracking signs can be taught and practised indoors, ready for the real thing when the rain stops.

Take the opportunity of the rain to start something new — a newsletter perhaps, or a logbook or scrapbook. Get ideas from the members for future activities — we spend so much time organising their events and meetings, do we really find the time to sit down and talk to them and find out what interests them? It's raining? Now's your chance!

RECORD KEEPING AND SAMPLE CHARTS

Programme planning is quite easy and gets easier, as long as you are organised about it. You should really plan on three levels — annually, monthly and week by week. Before the beginning of the year you should have some idea of the sort of things you wish to achieve in that time, the sort of significant commitments that you already have and an outline of themes and special activities you have in mind. From this skeleton, you can fatten out each month, preferably at a meeting with your helpers at least two weeks before that month begins, filling in details of activities, responsibilities, equipment etc. The weekly programme should be laid out in minute-by-minute detail including contingency plans for wet weather and similar hazards, and circulated to everybody involved in running the meeting, with their responsibilities clearly marked. As a guide, we have set out example programme formats for Annual, Monthly and Weekly programmes and for a camp. You will, four course, adapt them to suit your own situation. Having done so, we would suggest you draw up master grids of them and have a number copied, so you can fill them in as you go.

As important as planning in advance is record keeping afterwards. Although it is time consuming, it is worthwhile trying to sit down very soon after a meeting and making a note, on your planning chart, of what went well, what went badly and why. The charts can then be filed and, who knows, you might bring them out in four or five years' time and find some perfect, ready-made programmes, complete with lessons learned. You may have forgotten them. Your members will probably be a different set by then any way, so they can safely be trotted out, dusted off and run again, with the benefit of hindsight. As we said at the beginning — there is nothing new!

Weekly Programme

A minute by minute programme is something to drive at, even if it is seldom achieved on the night.

		Who	Equipment
6.30	Opening ceremony	DC	—
6.40	Rowdy game	LBJ	Ball
6.55	Quiet game	JB	Yoghurt tub etc.
7.00	Rowdy game	DC	Rope
7.15	Handcraft	ACF	Materials
7.40	Rowdy game	LBJ	Nil
7.50	Closing ceremony	DC	Nil
8.00	Go home	All!	

Monthly Programme

This should include the relevant information from the Annual Programme, plus fuller details of weekly outings and events. Preparation steps should be noted and responsibilities indicated.

WEEK 1	WEEK 2
— Carnival	— Planning Meeting
— Bank Holiday	—
—	—
—	—
— Meeting	— Meeting
—	—
—	—
WEEK 3	**WEEK 4**
—	—
—	— Set up base camp
—	—
—	— Camp
—	— Camp
— Meeting	— Camp

ANNUAL PROGRAMME PLANNER

Should include weekly meetings and themes, outings, special externally organised events you plan to attend, fund raising events, planning meetings, public holidays, school holidays, helpers' holidays.

JAN. Theme	FEB. Theme	MARCH Theme	APRIL Theme	MAY Theme	JUNE Theme
*	*	*	*	*	*
*	*	*	*	*	*
*	*	*	*	*	*
*	*	*	*	*	*

JULY Theme	AUG. Theme	SEPT. Theme	OCT. Theme	NOV. Theme	DEC. Theme
*	*	*	*	*	*
*	*	*	*	*	*
*	*	*	*	*	*
*	*	*	*	*	*

Camp Programme

A well-planned programme for a camp is vital. It allows you and your helpers to know exactly what should happen when, and it helps your members to feel a sense of continuity and stability. Contingency plans, especially for wet weather, should be written into the programme so that, should they be needed, they are readily available and are not just vague thoughts in your head. That is not the best place for them if you have to rush off to hospital with little Fred who has suspected appendicitis!

Timings		Where	Leader	Helpers	Equipment
	Friday				
7.30	Arrive 7.30				
7.45	Pitch tents				
8.45	Explore				
9.00	Drink & lights out				
	Saturday				
7.30	Rise				
8.00	Breakfast				
9.00	Sort out tents, bedding & kit				
9.45	Activity				
1.00	Lunch				
2.00	Activity				
4.00	Tea				
4.30	Activity				
6.00	Supper				
8.00	Camp Fire				
10.00	Lights out				
	Sunday				
8.00	Rise				
8.30	Breakfast				
9.30	Sort out tents, bedding & kit				
10.00	Religious Observation				
10.45	Activity				
1.00	Lunch				
2.00	Dismantle tents & pack up				
3.30	Activity				
4.15	Tea				
4.30	Depart				